*For my brother Rajeev, with whom I share
wonderful memories of feasting on delicious food
lovingly cooked by our mother, and who came up
with the idea of compiling our family favourites as a
tribute to her unconditional love*

*Each morning as I struggle to wake up
Aromas from the kitchen make me sit up.
I then follow my nose and watch my mother cook
Mouth-watering dishes though she never refers to a book.
She adds a pinch of this and a dash of that,
Ah yes! Plenty of love, no lack of that!*

SANJEEV KAPOOR

Mrs. Lata Lohana

AUTHOR'S NOTE

My mother is a great cook and I must give her all the credit for my cooking prowess. She not only raised my siblings and me with a lot of love, but also instilled in us her keen sense of taste and visual presentation. Since childhood I watched her churning out delicacy after delicacy in the kitchen, always mindful about what each one of us preferred. Simple food, with no extra frills, but absolutely delicious. Even today, cooking is not a hit or miss activity for her, even though she never refers to a written recipe. She does not measure the ingredients in cups or spoons. Years of experience have honed her skills to such an extent that each ingredient is added 'andaaz se'.

And when I got married to Alyona, another great cook stepped into my life – my mother-in-law. In the years to follow I was to discover her culinary expertise - she has this unique way of making traditional recipes extra special. Like the Vegetable Bhakarwadi or the Osaman which she makes with sabut moong instead of tuvar dal. Alyona recalls when they were children how she would come up with new ways of making the kids eat plenty of vegetables – she would cook them in such a way that they would devour willy-nilly whatever she put before them.

Our mothers helped us realise the advantages of home-cooked food. That one can be sure of getting fresh, healthy and nutritious food every day. Fresh food is richer in nutrients, in antioxidants, vitamins and micronutrients and all that is healthy and good. Daily cooking in each home allows for variety. Seasonal fresh fruits and vegetables

Mrs. Urmil Kapoor

get consumed. Less salt and preservatives are used. All hygiene precautions are taken. Vegetables, fruits, raw dals and rice are thoroughly washed and drained thus removing, to a large extent, any impurities and artificial colour and the pesticides in them. More than anything else, the quality and quantity of each ingredient that goes into the pan can be controlled.

My mother and mother-in-law's specialities are many, but due to space constraints. I could not include all of them in this book. Maybe a second volume? Actually that is not a bad idea at all. In fact, I think everyone should document their mothers' specialities. And I would certainly be happy to publish these jewels – Oh what a treasure that would make!! Till then I am confident that this collection of family recipes will be enjoyed by all.

Both my mother and mother-in-law are strict vegetarians hence all the recipes in this book are vegetarian. The recipes are for four portions keeping in mind that they will be part of a menu with other complimentary dishes. Both my mothers made all the dishes in our trial kitchen and as they cooked, my team documented the recipes and noted the amount of each ingredient as it was added to the pan. The recipes are now standardised and I can assure you that you can follow them blindly.

Happy Cooking !

CONTENTS

Beverages & Soups

MASALA DOODH

This recipe goes back a long way. In Alyona's Nana's home, they used to serve it as a special drink at Diwali and New Year. In her own home, my mother-in-law made a simpler version by powdering the almonds, pistachios and elaichi together and adding it to the milk to make a warm, nourishing winter drink for her little daughters.

Ingredients

A pinch of saffron

A pinch of nutmeg powder

¼ teaspoon green cardamom powder

15 almonds, blanched and coarsely ground

15 pistachios, blanched and coarsely ground

1 litre milk

5 tablespoons sugar

Method

1 Bring the milk to a boil in a deep non-stick pan. Lower the heat and simmer for about fifteen to twenty minutes, stirring continuously, till the milk reduces and thickens slightly.

2 Add the sugar and stir till it dissolves. Add the saffron, nutmeg powder and cardamom powder, and mix well. Simmer for another two to three minutes. Add the almonds and pistachios, and mix well. Serve hot or cold.

Surprise your guests by serving masala doodh in small glasses at Diwali, with a refreshing twist... chilled instead of warm!

GAJAR KI KANJI

This winter speciality, with its bright red colour and tangy,
mustardy flavour, is a must-serve at Holi at our home.

Ingredients

4 large carrots

1 large beetroot

2 tablespoons mustard seeds, coarsely powdered

1 tablespoons salt

1½ tablespoons coarse red chilli powder

Method

1 Scrub the carrots and beetroot and wash under running water. Peel and cut them into thin sticks.

2 Pour eighteen cups of water into a large jar or a clay pot (*matka*), with a capacity of five litres. Add the carrots, beetroot, powdered mustard, salt and chilli powder, and mix.

3 Cover the jar with a piece of muslin and fasten it around the rim with a piece of string. Stand the jar in direct sunlight for three to four days.

4 Place in a refrigerator to chill. Pour into tall glasses with some pieces of carrot and beetroot, and serve chilled.

Do not dilute the kanji with water to make it last longer, for both the colour and taste are lost. If it gets over, make a fresh lot.

AAM KA PANNA

Summer always means mangoes. The moment unripe mangoes appeared in the market my mother would make panna concentrate and store it in the refrigerator - a practice she follows till today. Just pour a couple of tablespoons into a glass, top it up with chilled water and serve – it is ever so refreshing.

Ingredients

1 kilogram unripe green mangoes

3 cups sugar

4 teaspoons roasted cumin powder

2 teaspoons black salt

Salt to taste

Do not make too much of the concentrate at one time as it loses its flavour.

Method

1 Wash and boil the mangoes and set aside to cool. Peel the mangoes; mash and strain the pulp.

2 Add five cups of water and mix well; cook till well blended.

3 Add the cumin powder, black salt, salt and sugar. Mix well and stir till the sugar dissolves. Remove from heat and set aside to cool. Chill in a refrigerator.

4 Pour the mango pulp into tall glasses and dilute with chilled water to taste. Serve immediately.

Chef's Tip: You can also dilute the *panna* concentrate with club soda instead of water.

SHIKANJAVI

The scent and flavour of freshly squeezed lemons makes this the ideal summer drink – cool and thirst-quenching. My mother always has a sugar syrup ready in the refrigerator. Whenever required she squeezes a lemon or two, adds the sugar syrup and tops it up with chilled water. Voilà – an instant refreshing drink!

Ingredients

1 cup lemon juice

3 cups sugar

1 tablespoon black salt

2 tablespoons roasted cumin powder

Club soda, as required (optional)

Shikanjavi syrup need not be stored in a refrigerator.

Method

1 Mix together the sugar, lemon juice, black salt and roasted cumin powder in a bottle and place it in direct sunlight for about six to seven days, or till the sugar dissolves completely. Shake the bottle once daily.

2 Pour two tablespoons of the syrup into a glass, top it up with one cup of chilled water or club soda, stir and serve immediately.

MIXED VEGETABLE SOUP

My mother-in-law has three daughters, and while they were growing up she was very particular about their nutrition. She also wanted to serve them something new and different everyday! One evening, she took out all the vegetables she could find in the refrigerator and used them to make a chunky vegetable soup. The kids wolfed it down with some fresh bread on the side. I am sure most kids will love it too.

Ingredients

1 medium carrot, finely chopped

¼ medium cabbage, finely chopped

1 medium potato, finely chopped

2 medium tomatoes, finely chopped

1 tablespoon butter

1 medium onion, finely chopped

1 tablespoon wholewheat flour

Salt to taste

Black pepper powder to taste

Method

1 Heat the butter in a deep non-stick pan and sauté the onion till translucent.

2 Add the chopped carrot, cabbage, potato and tomatoes, and stir to mix. Add the flour and cook, stirring, on medium heat for one or two minutes. Add the salt, pepper powder and four cups of water, and bring the mixture to a boil.

3 Lower the heat and simmer for five to seven minutes, or till all the vegetables are cooked. Serve piping hot.

MUSHROOM SOUP WITH ALMONDS

Mushrooms are an acquired taste. You either love them or hate them.
Either way, this simple soup, rich in flavour, will definitely be a hit at your table.

Ingredients

400 grams fresh button mushrooms, chopped

30 almonds

1 tablespoon butter

2 medium onions, finely chopped

5 cups milk

Salt to taste

White pepper powder to taste

Method

1 Blanch the almonds in one cup of hot water. Drain and peel; crush twenty almonds coarsely and cut the rest into thin slivers.

2 Heat the butter in a non-stick pan; add the onions and mushrooms, and sauté till they soften. Cool and process in a blender to make a smooth purée.

3 Transfer the purée to a non-stick pan; add the milk and mix well. Bring to a boil over medium heat. Add the crushed almonds, salt and pepper powder, and stir to mix. Serve piping hot, garnished with the almond slivers.

Chef's Tip: Do not wash or soak the mushrooms. Wipe them with a damp cloth.

Mrs. Urmil Kapoor

snacks & starters

VEGETABLE BHAKARWADI

My mother-in-law always used to find ready-made bhakarwadi very dry.
So one day when they had a party at home, she tried out a new recipe for
the filling using potatoes and other vegetables. They were a hit! Gradually
she learnt that she could make the spirals and keep them covered in the fridge
for up to two days and fry them when needed. A good thing, as she had to organise
many parties since my father-in-law was in the Navy and they socialised a lot.

Ingredients

100 grams shelled green peas

100 grams French beans, chopped roughly

3 potatoes, boiled and mashed

1 cup refined flour

1 tablespoon semolina

2 tablespoons oil + for deep-frying

Salt to taste

¼ teaspoon black pepper powder

½ cup chopped fresh coriander

½ cup grated coconut

2 teaspoons ginger-green chilli paste

1 teaspoon *garam masala* powder

Method

1 Mix together the flour, semolina, two tablespoons of oil, salt, pepper powder and sufficient water, and knead to make a semi-soft dough. Cover with a damp cloth and set aside.

2 Boil the green peas and French beans separately till soft. Drain thoroughly and mash.

3 Mix together the mashed green peas, French beans and potatoes, chopped coriander, coconut, ginger-green chilli paste, *garam masala* powder and salt.

4 Divide the dough into four equal portions and roll each one out into a thin *chapati*.

5 Spread the vegetable mixture evenly on all four *chapati*. Roll them up tightly into cylinders and cut the cylinders into half-inch thick slices.

6 Heat sufficient oil in a non-stick *kadai* and deep-fry the *bhakarwadi* on medium heat till golden brown and crisp. Drain on absorbent paper and serve.

Eat the bhakarwadi on the same day as they contain fresh vegetables.

Chef's Tip: If the mixture for the filling is too thin, add some beaten rice flakes and mix.

BESAN KE POODE

This is the ideal vegetarian substitute for omelettes. My father would make egg omelettes for us and himself, but since my mother is a vegetarian, she would make besan ke poode for herself, and we would polish that off as well.

Ingredients

2 cups gram flour

Salt to taste

½ teaspoon red chilli powder

3 medium onions, chopped

2-3 green chillies, chopped

2 tablespoons chopped fresh coriander

2 tablespoons oil

Method

1 Place the gram flour, salt, chilli powder, onions, green chillies and chopped coriander in a bowl. Add sufficient water to make a thick batter of dropping consistency.

2 Heat a non-stick *dosa tawa*; pour a ladleful of batter in the centre and spread it with the back of the ladle to form a thick *pooda*.

3 Drizzle a little oil all around. Flip the *pooda* and drizzle a little oil all around again. Cook till both sides are brown and crisp. Serve hot.

Makes 8 poode

CHANKI

This is a dish my mother-in-law learned from her aunt in Gujarat. And since it is so nutritious for kids she used to give them to her daughters regularly. And because it kept well, she used to make extra and reserve it for the kids' sudden demand for snacks.

Ingredients

1 cup *bajra* flour

2 tablespoons wholewheat flour

1½ tablespoons grated jaggery

½ cup yogurt

1 teaspoon carom seeds

½ teaspoon red chilli powder

½ teaspoon turmeric powder

Salt to taste

2 teaspoons oil + for shallow-frying

CHANKI

Method

1 Mix together both flours in a bowl.

2 Mix the jaggery with one-fourth cup of yogurt and whisk till the jaggery dissolves completely. Add to the flour mixture along with the carom seeds, chilli powder, turmeric powder, salt and two teaspoons of oil, and mix well. Add the remaining yogurt and knead into a semi-soft dough.

3 Divide the dough into eight equal portions and roll out each one into a thick *chapati*.

4 Heat a non-stick *tawa*, place a *chapati* on it and cook for a minute. Flip it over and drizzle a little oil all around. Cook till the underside is done. Flip it over again, drizzle a little more oil around and cook till both sides are evenly cooked. Serve hot.

Add fresh fenugreek to the dough for a special flavour.

BHAJANEE CHAKLI

When my mother-in-law was young, she used to make 100-200 chakli at one go, with her daughters helping her out as they enjoyed using the mould. Then they would pack the chakli up in polythene bags and gift them to their friends and relatives at Diwali. Chakli, chivda and laddoo … three Diwali specials at our home. Even now her nieces, nephews and some of their friends' children call her from all over the world to ask her to send them her famous chakli.

Ingredients

Bhajanee Flour

4 cups rice

1 cup skinless split black gram

Dough

2 cups *bhajanee* flour

2 tablespoons butter

Salt to taste

1 teaspoon cumin powder

1 teaspoon red chilli powder

Oil for deep-frying

Add 1 teaspoon of sesame seeds to the dough for special occasions.

Method

1 For the *bhajanee* flour, dry-roast the rice and black gram separately. Cool completely and grind separately to a powder. Sift both the flours and mix.

2 Place two cups of *bhajanee* flour in a bowl. Add the butter, salt, cumin powder and chilli powder, and mix well. Divide the mixture in half.

3 Take one half and knead into a soft dough with half a cup of water. When the dough is used up, make a dough of the remaining flour.

4 Put small portions of the mixture into a *chakli* mould and press out several *chakli* onto a plastic sheet.

5 Heat sufficient oil in a non-stick *kadai* till moderately hot. Deep-fry the *chakli* till light golden brown and crisp. Drain on absorbent paper and set aside to cool. Store in an airtight container.

PYAAZ–TAMATAR KA BUN

As children we always wanted to eat something different when we returned home ravenous from school. One evening my mother tried this recipe as an alternative to bun omelettes and it was hit. Now all her grandchildren clamour for it.

Ingredients

2 medium onions, sliced

5 medium tomatoes, sliced

2 tablespoons oil

Salt to taste

½ teaspoon red chilli powder

½ teaspoon *garam masala* powder

2 teaspoons sugar

8 *pav*

2 tablespoons pure ghee

Method

1 Heat the oil in a non-stick pan; add the onions and sauté till translucent.

2 Add the tomatoes, salt, chilli powder and *garam masala* powder, and sauté till cooked.

3 Add the sugar and sauté till the tomatoes are completely soft and pulpy.

4 Divide the mixture into eight equal portions. Slit the *pav* and fill with the onion-tomato mixture.

5 Heat a non-stick *tawa*; place the stuffed *pav* on it, one or two at a time, and drizzle a little ghee all around. Cook till lightly browned and crisp. Serve hot.

TEEN DAL KE DAHI BHALLE

My mother first tasted this dish at a relative's home and enjoyed it thoroughly.
It was somewhat like the popular dahi ke bhalle yet it had a distinctive flavour and taste.
She asked them for the recipe, tried it out successfully at home and it has
been a family favourite ever since.

Ingredients

½ cup skinless split green gram

½ cup skinless split black gram

2 tablespoons split Bengal gram

Salt to taste

1 teaspoon green chilli paste

1½ teaspoons red chilli powder

2 tablespoons finely chopped
    fresh coriander

Oil for deep-frying

2½ cups yogurt, whisked and chilled

½ cup milk

½ teaspoon rock salt

1 teaspoon roasted cumin powder

4 tablespoons Tamarind Chutney
    (page 91)

½ cup Green Chutney (page 91)

Method

1 Mix together and soak all the lentils in four cups of water for three to four hours. Drain and grind, using very little water, to a slightly coarse paste.

2 Add the salt, green chilli paste, one-fourth teaspoon chilli powder and one tablespoon chopped coriander. Mix well with your hand to make a fluffy mixture. Add about one tablespoon of water if the batter is too thick.

3 Bring some water to a boil in a pan. Heat sufficient oil in a non-stick *kadai*. Moisten your fingers and drop small portions of the batter into the oil. Deep-fry, on medium heat, till golden brown. Drain the *bhalle* and soak in the boiling water for ten minutes.

4 Place the chilled yogurt in a bowl. Add half a cup of milk and whisk well till smooth. Add salt, one-fourth teaspoon chilli powder and the rock salt, and mix well. Add a little more milk if the yogurt is too thick.

5 Take the *bhalle* out of the boiling water and soak them in water at room temperature for ten minutes. Squeeze out the excess water and place the *bhalle* in a serving bowl.

6 Pour the yogurt on top of the *bhalle* and sprinkle roasted cumin powder, the remaining chilli powder, tamarind chutney, green chutney and the remaining chopped coriander on top.

Main Dishes

BHARWAN TINDA

*The delicate balance of spices gives this dish its characteristic flavour. The tinda grown
in the north is especially tasty, which is why my brother, sister and I love this dish.
And when my mother cooks it, it becomes even more special.*

Ingredients

500 grams round gourd *(tinda)*

1 teaspoon turmeric powder

4 teaspoons coriander powder

1½ teaspoons red chilli powder

Salt to taste

¼ cup oil

1 teaspoon cumin seeds

1 medium onion, chopped

1 tablespoon ginger-garlic paste

2 medium tomatoes, chopped

1 tablespoon chopped fresh coriander

Method

1 Wash the *tinda* and wipe them dry. Slice off both ends and scrape off the thick skin. Slit each *tinda* into four without separating the pieces.

2 Mix together half a teaspoon turmeric powder, three teaspoons coriander powder, one teaspoon chilli powder and salt to taste. Stuff the slit *tinda* with the mixture.

3 Heat the oil in a pressure cooker. Add the cumin seeds and sauté till they change colour. Add the onion and ginger-garlic paste and sauté for two to three minutes on medium heat.

4 Add the tomatoes and sauté till soft and pulpy. Add the remaining turmeric, coriander and chilli powders, and stir well to mix. If the mixture is too dry, sprinkle a little water and sauté for a minute or two.

5 Add the stuffed *tinda* and sauté for three to four minutes. Add one cup of water and bring the mixture to a boil. Seal the cooker with the lid and cook till the pressure is released twice (two whistles).

6 Remove the lid when the pressure has reduced completely. Serve hot, garnished with the chopped coriander.

ALOO WADI

For this dish, spicy Amritsari wadi are the best. Relatives residing in Amritsar visit us bearing gifts of the famed Amritsari wadi, which they know will be much appreciated.

Ingredients

2 large (100 grams) dried
   urad dal nuggets (*wadi*)

4 medium potatoes

2 medium onions, roughly chopped

2 inches ginger, roughly chopped

3 tablespoons oil

½ teaspoon cumin seeds

2 large tomatoes, puréed

1 teaspoon turmeric powder

2 teaspoons coriander powder

½ teaspoon cumin powder

½ teaspoon red chilli powder

Salt to taste

¼ teaspoon *garam masala* powder

1 tablespoon chopped fresh coriander

Method

1 Break the nuggets into small pieces. Peel and quarter the potatoes lengthways. Grind the onions and ginger to a fine paste.

2 Heat the oil in a pressure cooker and add the cumin seeds. When they begin to change colour, add the onion-ginger paste and sauté for three minutes.

3 Crush and add the nuggets and continue to sauté for five minutes, sprinkling a little water whenever the mixture turns a little dry.

4 Add the tomato purée and sauté till the oil rises to the surface. Add the turmeric powder, coriander powder, cumin powder, chilli powder and salt, and mix well. Add the potatoes and sauté for two minutes.

5 Stir in two cups of water and bring to a boil. Seal the cooker with its lid and cook till the pressure is released two to three times (two to three whistles).

6 Remove the lid when the pressure has reduced completely. Sprinkle the *garam masala* powder and chopped coriander, and serve hot.

BAINGAN KA BHARTA

*Baingan ka bharta is an integral part of a traditional Punjabi menu.
My mother uses a lot of onions in her recipe. Their sweetness not only
adds to the taste, but also gives the dish a wonderful texture.*

Ingredients

1 large brinjal

3 tablespoons oil

5 large onions, chopped

3 medium tomatoes, chopped

Salt to taste

1 teaspoon red chilli powder

2 tablespoons chopped fresh coriander

Method

1 Roast the brinjal on a medium flame till well cooked and the skin has charred completely. Cool, peel and mash.

2 Heat the oil in a non-stick pan and sauté the onions till light golden brown. Add the tomatoes, salt and chilli powder, and sauté till the *masala* is cooked and the oil rises to the surface.

3 Add the mashed brinjal and mix well. Lower the heat and cook for four to five minutes. Add the chopped coriander and mix well. Serve hot.

Add a quarter cup of grated
cauliflower or boiled green
peas while sautéing the onions
as a variation.

BOONDI KI SABZI

This is a jhatphat recipe, which is ideal to whip up for unexpected guests.
My mother always keeps boondi in stock for just such an eventuality.
But she also cooks this dish for her grandchildren who love it.

Ingredients

250 grams unsalted *boondi*

1 tablespoon oil

½ teaspoon cumin seeds

A large pinch of asafoetida

4-5 spring onions with greens, chopped

¼ teaspoon turmeric powder

1 teaspoon red chilli powder

1 teaspoon coriander powder

Salt to taste

1 tablespoon chopped fresh coriander

Method

1 Heat the oil in a non-stick pan. Add the cumin seeds and when they begin to change colour, add the asafoetida and spring onions. Sauté till lightly coloured.

2 Add the turmeric powder, chilli powder and coriander powder, and sauté till fragrant.

3 Add the *boondi* and salt, and stir to mix well. Add a quarter cup of water and simmer for two to three minutes.

4 Garnish with the chopped coriander and serve immediately.

MOOLI AUR PATTE KI SABZI

The abundance of mooli available in Delhi in winter got my mother-in-law wondering what new dish to make with them. She started cooking them and their leaves lightly with onion and spices. This is still my father-in-law's favourite dish as long as it is made fresh and served straight from the stove.

Ingredients

4 medium white radishes with leaves
2 tablespoons oil
1 teaspoon mustard seeds
2 green chillies, chopped
A pinch of asafoetida
Salt to taste
4-5 spring onions, chopped
½ teaspoon red chilli powder
¼ teaspoon turmeric powder
2 tablespoons roasted gram flour

Method

1 Cut the radishes lengthways into four, and then into thin slices. Chop the leaves.

2 Heat the oil in a non-stick pan; add the mustard seeds, green chillies and asafoetida. When the seeds begin to splutter, add the radish and mix.

3 Cover and cook on medium heat for two to three minutes. Add salt and mix well.

4 Add the radish leaves and spring onions, and stir. Cover and cook on medium heat till tender. Add the chilli powder and turmeric powder, and sauté for two to three minutes.

5 Sprinkle the gram flour and sauté for two to three minutes. Serve hot.

PANEER BHURJI

No Punjabi kitchen is complete without paneer. This versatile ingredient can be turned into a mouth-watering dish in a jiffy. This is one of my brother Rajeev's favourite dishes.

Ingredients

400 grams cottage cheese
3 tablespoons oil
2 teaspoons cumin seeds
3-4 green chillies, slit
4 medium onions, chopped
½ teaspoon turmeric powder
½ teaspoon red chilli powder
Salt to taste
2 tablespoons chopped fresh coriander

Method

1 Heat the oil in a non-stick pan; add the cumin seeds and green chillies. When the seeds begin to change colour, add the onions and sauté till light brown. Add the turmeric powder, chilli powder and salt, and stir well to mix.

2 Crumble the cottage cheese and add to the pan and mix well. Cook for two to three minutes, stirring lightly. Serve hot, garnished with the chopped coriander.

Chef's Tip: Add peas for extra flavour and colour.

KARELE KI SABZI

My mother always scrapes the outer skin of the karela and instead of discarding it, uses it in the dish.
She believes that the real flavour and nutrients of the vegetable lie in the outer skin.
The only precaution is that it should be very well sautéed to reduce the bitterness.
This dish is a great favourite with my office colleagues.

Ingredients

5-6 medium bitter gourds *(karele)*

2 tablespoons salt + to taste

3 tablespoons oil + for deep-frying

2 medium onions, sliced

2 teaspoons coriander powder

1 teaspoon dried mango powder

1 teaspoon red chilli powder

Method

1 Scrape the bitter gourds and reserve the scrapings. Slit each one vertically and remove the seeds.

2 Rub two tablespoons of salt all over the bitter gourds and the scrapings, keeping them separate.

3 Set aside for two hours. Wash thoroughly and squeeze dry.

4 Heat sufficient oil in a non-stick *kadai* and deep-fry the bitter gourds till dark brown. Drain on absorbent paper.

5 Heat three tablespoons of oil in a non-stick pan; add the bitter gourd scrapings and sauté till brown.

6 Add the onions and sauté for two to three minutes. Add the coriander powder, dried mango powder and chilli powder, and sauté for another minute or two.

7 Add the fried bitter gourd, and more salt if necessary. Cover and cook for two to three minutes. Serve hot.

Rubbing salt on bitter gourds removes the bitterness to a great extent. Wash thoroughly before using.

BHARWAN ARBI

According to my Nani, bharwan arbi tasted best when my mother made it.
So whenever the dish was on the menu, she would insist that my mother prepare it.
And now all her great-grandchildren enjoy it.

Ingredients

400 grams colocasia tubers

1 teaspoon red chilli powder

2 teaspoons coriander powder

½ teaspoon turmeric powder

2 teaspoons dried mango powder

1 teaspoon *garam masala* powder

Salt to taste

3 tablespoons oil

1 tablespoon chopped fresh coriander

Method

1 Peel and make a slit in each colocasia tuber without cutting through.

2 Mix together the chilli powder, coriander powder, turmeric powder, dried mango powder, *garam masala* powder and salt. Stuff the mixture into the slits in the colocasia. Reserve the remaining *masala*.

3 Heat the oil in a pressure cooker; add the colocasia and sauté till lightly browned.

4 Sprinkle the remaining *masala* and mix. Add half a cup of water and seal the cooker with its lid and cook under pressure till the pressure is released once (one whistle).

5 Remove the lid when the pressure has reduced completely. Garnish with the chopped coriander and serve hot.

FRENCH BEAN SABZI

This is a favourite at my in-laws' home. Because party food is usually heavy, my mother-in-law makes it a point to serve this lovely crunchy green vegetable dish. It is delicious with hot roti!

Ingredients

300 grams French beans, finely chopped

1 tablespoon oil

½ teaspoon mustard seeds

A pinch of asafoetida

1½ teaspoons ginger-green chilli paste

Salt to taste

A pinch of soda bicarbonate

1 tablespoon chopped fresh coriander

1 tablespoon grated coconut

A dash of fresh lemon juice

Method

1 Heat the oil in a non-stick pan. Add the mustard seeds and when they begin to splutter, add the asafoetida and ginger-green chilli paste. Stir, add the French beans and mix well.

2 Add the salt and soda bicarbonate, and stir to mix. Sprinkle one-fourth cup of water and cook, uncovered, on medium heat, for five to seven minutes, or till the beans soften but are still crunchy.

3 Garnish with the chopped coriander, grated coconut and a dash of lemon, and serve.

KAMAL KAKDI KE KOFTE

It is a bit tedious to make these kofte but the end result is well worth all that effort. The kamal kakdi should be cleaned thoroughly. Soak them in water for some time and then scrub them well. My mother recalls that during her schooldays, she would use a pin to remove the mud from the crevices till my Nani told her to soak them for a while and then clean them.

Ingredients

Kofte	Gravy
250 grams lotus root	2 medium onions, roughly chopped
1 large potato	1½ inches ginger, roughly chopped
3½ tablespoons gram flour	2 tablespoons oil
1 tablespoon cornflour	½ teaspoon turmeric powder
¼ teaspoon red chilli powder	1 teaspoon red chilli powder
1½ teaspoons crushed dried pomegranate seeds	1 tablespoon coriander powder
	2 medium tomatoes, puréed
Salt to taste	Salt to taste
Oil for deep-frying	½ teaspoon *garam masala* powder
	2 tablespoons chopped fresh coriander

Method

1 Scrub and wash the lotus roots thoroughly; peel and grate. Grate the potato and soak in water for two to three minutes. Drain and squeeze to remove excess water. Place both the lotus root and potato in a blender and process for a minute.

2 Transfer the mixture to a bowl. Add the gram flour, cornflour, chilli powder, crushed pomegranate seeds and salt, and mix well. Divide the mixture into twelve portions and shape each portion into a round *kofta*.

3 Heat sufficient oil in a non-stick *kadai* and deep-fry the *kofte* till golden. Drain on absorbent paper.

4 For the gravy, grind the onions and ginger to a fine paste. Heat the oil in a non-stick pan; add the onion-ginger paste and sauté until light golden brown. Add the turmeric powder, chilli powder and coriander powder. Cook on medium heat for one minute, stirring continuously.

5 Stir in the tomato purée and cook on high heat, stirring continuously, till the oil rises to the surface. Add one and a half cups of water and bring the gravy to a boil. Add the salt, lower the heat and simmer for five minutes.

6 Add the *kofte* and simmer for two minutes. Sprinkle the *garam masala* powder and serve hot, garnished with the chopped coriander.

Chef's Tip: Choose lotus roots which have both ends closed.

BHARWAN BHINDI

This is our family's favourite bhindi recipe. The amchur is the key ingredient as it helps prevent stickiness and also adds a delightfully tangy flavour.

Ingredients

250 grams ladies' fingers

1 teaspoon red chilli powder

2 tablespoons coriander powder

1 teaspoon cumin powder

2 teaspoons dried mango powder

1 teaspoon turmeric powder

1 teaspoon *garam masala* powder

Salt to taste

4-5 shallots, slit

2 tablespoons oil

Method

1 Wash and wipe the ladies' fingers completely dry. Trim and make a vertical slit only on one side of each one and set aside.

2 Mix together the chilli powder, coriander powder, cumin powder, dried mango powder, turmeric powder, *garam masala* powder and salt in a bowl.

3 Stuff the ladies' fingers and the shallots with the *masala*. Reserve the remaining *masala*. Heat the oil in a non-stick *kadai*. Add the stuffed ladies' fingers and shallots, and stir.

4 Sprinkle the reserved *masala*. Cook, covered, on low heat for eight to ten minutes stirring occasionally. Cover the pan and cook till tender. Serve hot.

Chef's Tip: Do not add any water while cooking, or the vegetable will become sticky.

BHEN KI SABZI

My father was very fond of this vegetable but my mother wasn't aware of it for a long time till she served the dish for guests. My father said to her, "How come you don't cook this dish for me? I love it so much." Since then, to his great delight, the dish regularly appeared at their table.

Ingredients

250 grams lotus roots

2 large potatoes, cut into 1-inch pieces

2 tablespoons oil

2 medium onions, chopped

1½ teaspoons ginger paste

½ teaspoon turmeric powder

2 teaspoons coriander powder

1 teaspoon red chilli powder

Salt to taste

1 large tomato, chopped

A pinch of *garam masala* powder

1 tablespoon chopped fresh coriander

Method

1 Scrub and wash the lotus roots thoroughly. Peel and cut them into diagonal slices.

2 Heat the oil in a pressure cooker. Add the onions and sauté till lightly browned. Add the ginger paste and sauté for a few minutes. Add the turmeric powder, coriander powder, chilli powder and salt. Add a little water if the mixture is too dry. Sauté the mixture till the oil rises to the surface.

3 Add the lotus roots and potatoes, and mix well. Add half a cup of water and seal the cooker with the lid. Cook under pressure till the pressure is released three to four times (three to four whistles). Remove the lid when the pressure has reduced completely.

4 Add the tomato and cover the cooker again and cook till the pressure is released once (one whistle). Alternatively, cook on low heat till both the lotus root and tomato are soft.

5 When the pressure reduces, remove the lid and cook till the gravy reduces and thickens. Sprinkle the *garam masala* powder, garnish with the chopped coriander and serve hot.

DAHI KI SABZI

This is another one of those quick-fix dishes which is easy to turn out as Punjabi households are usually well-stocked with yogurt.

Ingredients

2½ cups fresh yogurt

2 teaspoons oil

1 teaspoon cumin seeds

1 medium onion, chopped

1 green chilli, slit

¾ teaspoon turmeric powder

¼ teaspoon red chilli powder

1 teaspoon coriander powder

Salt to taste

¼ teaspoon *garam masala* powder

1 tablespoon chopped fresh coriander

Method

1 Heat the oil in a non-stick *kadai*. Add the cumin seeds and sauté till they begin to change colour. Add the onion and green chilli, and sauté till the onion turns light brown.

2 Add the turmeric powder, chilli powder and coriander powder, and stir. Add the yogurt and salt, and stir lightly. Add the *garam masala* powder and mix well.

3 Remove from heat, garnish with the chopped coriander and serve hot with *roti*.

You can make this dish with fresh malai as well. It is richer and absolutely delicious!

KATHAL KI SABZI

Some call it 'vegetarian mutton'. Deep-fry the kathal for best results.
And yes, cook it with yogurt for that rich 'shahi' taste.

Ingredients

500 grams unripe jackfruit

2 tablespoons oil + for deep-frying

2 medium potatoes, cut into
   1-inch cubes

4 medium onions

1 inch ginger

¼ teaspoon turmeric powder

½ teaspoon red chilli powder

1½ teaspoons coriander powder

1 cup yogurt

Salt to taste

1 teaspoon Punjabi *Garam Masala*
   Powder (see below)

2 tablespoons chopped fresh coriander

Method

1 Apply a tablespoon of oil to your palms and to the knife. Remove the thick skin and the centre core of the jackfruit. Cut the jackfruit into one-inch cubes.

2 Heat sufficient oil in a non-stick *kadai* and deep-fry the jackfruit cubes till golden. Drain on absorbent paper. In the same oil, deep-fry the potato cubes till golden. Drain.

3 Grind the onions and ginger to a fine paste.

4 Heat two tablespoons of oil in a non-stick pan. Add the onion-ginger paste and sauté till lightly coloured. Add the turmeric powder, chilli powder and coriander powder. Stir and add two tablespoons of water to prevent the *masala* from scorching and continue to sauté till fragrant.

5 Add the yogurt and two tablespoons of water, and sauté till the oil rises to the surface.

6 Add the jackfruit, potato cubes and salt, and mix well. Lower the heat and cook for two to three minutes. Add the Punjabi *garam masala* powder and mix lightly. Garnish with the chopped coriander and serve hot.

PUNJABI GARAM MASALA POWDER

Dry-roast 100 grams black peppercorns, 100 grams cumin seeds, 10 grams black cardamoms, 4-5 cloves and 1 inch cinnamon separately. Cool and grind all the spices together to a powder.

JEERA ALOO

In our home the jeera aloo is made a little differently from the one you find in most other homes or restaurants. We like it 'latpata', meaning the potato cubes are well covered with masala. The trick is to sauté the potatoes well to get that special texture, flavour and colour.

Ingredients

1 teaspoon cumin seeds

1 teaspoon roasted cumin powder

4 large potatoes, boiled and
    cut into 1-inch cubes

4 tablespoons oil

Salt to taste

1 teaspoon red chilli powder

1 tablespoon coriander seeds, crushed

2 teaspoons dried mango powder

2 tablespoons chopped fresh coriander

Method

1 Heat the oil in a non-stick pan. Add the cumin seeds and sauté till they change colour.

2 Add the salt and stir. Add the chilli powder, crushed coriander seeds, roasted cumin powder and dried mango powder, and stir to mix well.

3 Add the potato cubes and sauté carefully till the *masala* coats the potato cubes well. Add the chopped coriander and stir. Serve hot.

LAUKI KE KOFTE

The uniqueness of these kofte lies in the fact that they are stuffed with pieces of tamarind with the seeds in them. The tamarind gives it a tangy flavour while the seeds help retain the shape of the kofte.

Ingredients

Kofte

750 grams bottle gourd

5 tablespoons gram flour

½ teaspoon red chilli powder

Salt to taste

12 pieces of tamarind with seeds

Oil for deep-frying

½ teaspoon *garam masala* powder

2 tablespoons chopped fresh coriander

Gravy

3 tablespoons oil

2 medium onions, chopped

5 medium tomatoes, puréed

¾ teaspoon turmeric powder

¾ teaspoon red chilli powder

1½ tablespoons coriander powder

Salt to taste

Method

1 For the *kofte*, peel and grate the bottle gourd. Squeeze to remove excess water. Add the gram flour, chilli powder and salt, and mix well. Divide the mixture into twelve equal portions.

2 Stuff one piece of tamarind into each portion and shape into a round *kofta*. Remove the tamarind seeds if desired.

3 Heat sufficient oil in a non-stick *kadai* and deep-fry the *kofte*, in small batches, for two to three minutes, or until golden brown and crisp on the outside. Drain on absorbent paper and set aside.

4 For the gravy, heat the oil in a non-stick pan; add the onions and sauté until light golden brown. Add the tomato purée and cook till the oil rises to the surface.

5 Add the turmeric powder, chilli powder and coriander powder. Continue to sauté on medium heat for one minute. Add two tablespoons of water and sauté till the oil rises to the surface again.

6 Add two cups of water and bring to a boil. Add the salt, lower the heat and simmer for five minutes. Keep the gravy hot.

7 To serve, arrange the *kofte* on a serving platter and pour the gravy over them. Sprinkle *garam masala* powder and garnish with the chopped coriander.

Instead of tamarind, you can stuff the kofte with dried plums or dried pomegranate seeds.

SARSON KA SAAG

*This is the most famous Punjabi dish and an all-time Punjabi favourite. My mother always boils
the greens so that they are soft and completely cooked. She insists this enhances the taste.*

Ingredients

1 kilogram fresh mustard leaves

200 grams spinach

200 grams *bathua*

2 tablespoons cornmeal

3-4 tablespoons pure ghee

2 medium onions, finely chopped

2 inches ginger, finely chopped

6-8 garlic cloves, chopped

4 green chillies, finely chopped

Salt to taste

Butter to serve

Method

1 Trim the stems of the mustard leaves, spinach and *bathua*. Chop the leaves and any
tender stems. Boil the greens together with one-fourth cup of water till well cooked and
yellowish in colour. If there is any water left, strain and reserve.

2 Grind the leaves and stems to a paste. Add the cornmeal and mix. Heat the ghee in a
non-stick pan. Add the onions, ginger, garlic and green chillies, and sauté till lightly
browned.

3 Add the ground leaves and sauté for five to six minutes. Add salt and the reserved water
to adjust the consistency if required, and continue to cook, stirring, for four to five
minutes or till well blended. Serve hot with butter and *makki ki roti*.

Traditionally sarson ka saag is
pounded to a paste with a wooden
mathni or ravai, while it is being
cooked. The process is quite
cumbersome and time-consuming,
but the result is delicious.

QUICK PRESSURE-COOKED VEGETABLES

My mother usually makes this for breakfast and serves it with bread or toast. In our home we like to have something different for breakfast everyday and this is very quick to make and very healthy.

Ingredients

2 medium potatoes, cut into ½-inch pieces and soaked in water

¾ cup shelled green peas

3 medium carrots, cut into ½-inch pieces

1 teaspoon oil

A pinch of *garam masala* powder

Salt to taste

A pinch of *chaat masala*

½ teaspoon black pepper powder

Method

1 Heat the oil in a pressure cooker; add the *garam masala* powder, salt, *chaat masala* and pepper powder, and stir. Add the potatoes, green peas, carrots, and one tablespoon of water.

2 Cover and cook under pressure till the pressure is released once (one whistle). Remove from heat.

3 Once the pressure reduces, remove the lid and serve immediately.

UNDHIYO

This is one my favourite dishes and my mother-in-law makes it best. When I visit my in-laws in Pune, I go loaded with fresh papdi, kand and other vegetables and request her to cook it for me. So popular is her undhiyo, that while posted in Delhi, one of her friends even flew in papdi from Gujarat just to learn how to make the dish, and guests invited to her parties have called up beforehand to enquire whether Undhiyo would be on the menu!

Ingredients

250 grams *Surti papdi*

100 grams fresh *papdi dana*

4-5 small brinjals

4-5 medium potatoes, halved

250 grams purple yam, cut into ¾-inch cubes

250 grams yam, cut into ¾-inch cubes

1 unripe banana, cut into ¾-inch cubes

2 pinches of soda bicarbonate

Salt to taste

1 cup grated coconut

1 cup green garlic, chopped

2 cups chopped fresh coriander

1 teaspoon coriander powder

1½ teaspoons green chilli-ginger paste

½ cup shelled green peas

3 tablespoons oil

1 teaspoon carom seeds

Muthiya

¼ cup gram flour

½ cup wholewheat flour

1 cup fenugreek leaves, chopped

A pinch of soda bicarbonate

Salt to taste

1 teaspoon ginger-green chilli paste

2 teaspoons coriander powder

¼ teaspoon turmeric powder

1 teaspoon red chilli powder

2 teaspoons oil + for deep-frying

Yogurt, as required

Method

1. Trim the *Surti papdi* and slit them open. Add the *papdi dana*, a pinch of soda bicarbonate and a little salt, mix well and set aside.

2. To make the *muthiya*, add a pinch of soda bicarbonate and salt to the fenugreek leaves, mix well and set aside for five minutes.

3. Mix together the gram flour, wholewheat flour, fenugreek leaves, ginger-green chilli paste, coriander powder, turmeric powder, chilli powder and salt with two teaspoons of oil and enough yogurt, to make a stiff dough.

4. Divide the dough into small portions and shape each one into a one-inch long and half-inch thick roll.

5. Heat sufficient oil in a non-stick *kadai* and deep-fry the rolls on medium heat till golden brown. Drain on absorbent paper and set aside.

6 Slit the brinjals into four without cutting through the stem. Mix together all the vegetables with a little salt and a pinch of soda bicarbonate, and set aside.

7 Mix together the coconut, green garlic, chopped coriander, coriander powder, green chilli-ginger paste and salt. Grind half the coconut mixture with the peas to a paste. Add the remaining coconut mixture and mix well.

8 Add half the coconut-pea mixture to the *surti papad* and papdi dana and mix. Add the remaining coconut-pea mixture to the other vegetables and mix.

9 Heat the oil in a thick-bottomed non-stick pan; add the carom seeds and sauté till fragrant. Add two cups of water and bring the mixture to a boil. Place alternate layers of the surti papdi and mixed vegetables in the pan.

10 Lower the heat, cover and cook till the vegetables are almost tender. Occasionally, stir the vegetables gently. Lastly, add the fried *muthiya* and continue to cook, covered, for five minutes. Serve hot with *puri* or *chapati*.

Notes: 1) *Surti papdi* is a variety of broad beans.
2) *Papdi dana* are shelled beans.

The secret of making a successful undhiyo is to prepare some parts of it like the muthiya the previous day. Another tip - use less oil and more water for a healthy version of this dish.

VEGETABLE DHANSAAK

When my father-in-law was posted in Vishakapatnam, they had a Parsi friend who taught my mother-in-law how to make mutton dhansaak with brown rice. There are some perks to being in the services - travel far and wide, make new friends and learn about different cuisines! Dhansaak, as my mother-in-law discovered when she turned vegetarian twenty-five years ago, can be made with vegetables too.

Ingredients

¼ cup split pigeon peas, soaked

2 tablespoons split red lentils, soaked

2 tablespoons skinless split green gram, soaked

2 tablespoons split Bengal gram, soaked

100 grams red pumpkin, cut into ½-inch cubes

2 medium brinjals, cut into ½-inch cubes

1 large potato, cut into ½-inch cubes

65 grams fenugreek leaves, chopped

10-15 fresh mint leaves, chopped

½ teaspoon turmeric powder

Salt to taste

1 inch ginger, chopped

5–6 garlic cloves, chopped

4-5 green chillies

1 teaspoon cumin seeds

2 tablespoons pure ghee

2 tablespoons oil

2 medium onions, chopped

2 medium tomatoes, chopped

2 tablespoons *dhansaak masala*

1 teaspoon red chilli powder

2 tablespoons lemon juice

2 tablespoons chopped fresh coriander

Method

1 Drain and mix all the lentils together in a pressure cooker. Add four cups of water, the pumpkin, brinjals, potato, fenugreek leaves, mint leaves, turmeric power and salt, and cook under pressure till the pressure is released four times (four whistles).

2 Remove the lid of the cooker when the pressure has reduced completely. Whisk the mixture till smooth.

3 Grind together the ginger, garlic, green chillies, cumin seeds and a little salt to a fine paste.

4 Heat the ghee and oil in a deep non-stick pan. Add the onions and sauté till golden. Add the tomatoes and sauté till soft.

5 Add the ground paste and continue to sauté till fragrant. Add the *dhansaak masala* and chilli powder, and mix well.

6 Add the *dal* and vegetables, and mix. Adjust the salt and cook on low heat for five minutes.

7 Add the lemon juice and chopped coriander and mix. Serve hot with brown rice.

Rice & Roti

LEMON RICE WITH VEGETABLES

My mother-in-law used to sometimes find cooking dinner a bit of a chore, so she would cook extra rice in the morning, and cook the leftover rice with different seasonings for the evening meal. Her lemon rice with vegetables added for more nutrition, was a particular favourite with her three daughters, who loved anything their mother cooked for them.

Ingredients

2 tablespoons lemon juice

2 cups cooked rice

1 small carrot, grated

1 small green capsicum, chopped

2 tablespoons oil

¼ teaspoon mustard seeds

A pinch of asafoetida

2 green chillies, chopped

15-20 curry leaves

2 dried red chillies, broken into large bits

1 small onion, finely chopped

¼ teaspoon turmeric powder

¼ cup roasted peanuts, crushed (optional)

Salt to taste

Method

1 Heat the oil in a non-stick *kadai*. Add the mustard seeds, asafoetida, green chillies, curry leaves and red chillies. When the seeds begin to splutter, add the onion and sauté till translucent.

2 Add the carrot and capsicum, and sauté for four to five minutes. Add the rice, turmeric powder, roasted peanuts, salt and lemon juice, and mix well. Cook till the rice is heated through. Serve hot.

ALOO PALAK PULAO

As children we did not like palak, so my mother devised this delicious recipe to make sure we would eat this healthy leafy vegetable. Of course the presence of potato, which is a hot favourite with most children, helps. And so does the beautiful green colour that spinach adds to the pulao.

Ingredients

2 medium potatoes, cut into ¾-inch cubes

1 cup finely chopped spinach

1½ cups rice, soaked

2 tablespoons ghee

1 teaspoon cumin seeds

1 medium tomato, finely chopped

¼ medium (125 grams) bottle gourd, peeled and cut into ¾-inch cubes

Salt to taste

Method

1 Heat the ghee in a deep non-stick pan and add the cumin seeds. When they begin to change colour, add the tomato, potatoes and bottle gourd, and sauté for two minutes.

2 Add the rice and spinach, and sauté for two more minutes. Add three cups of hot water and salt, and mix.

3 When the mixture comes to a boil, lower heat, cover and cook till the rice and vegetables are tender. Serve hot.

QUICK SICHUAN RICE

This is my mother-in-law's own creation that needs only cabbage, carrot and vinegar. She was not comfortable serving plain rice or jeera rice at parties so she came up with this simple and quick solution. Her guests enjoyed it and compliments were showered on her!

Ingredients

2 cups cooked rice

2 dried red chillies

1 teaspoon crushed red chillies

2 tablespoons vinegar

2 tablespoons oil

4-5 garlic cloves, chopped

1 medium onion, chopped

¼ small cabbage, grated

1 medium carrot, grated

Salt to taste

Method

1 Soak the dried chillies in vinegar for about half an hour. Drain and reserve the vinegar.

2 Heat the oil in a non-stick wok. Add the garlic, onion, crushed red chillies, drained red chillies, cabbage and carrot, and sauté on medium heat for about five minutes.

3 Add the rice, reserved vinegar and salt; toss well to mix.

4 Serve immediately.

IMLI CHAWAL

This is one of my mother's favourite recipes. She learnt it from Amma, an elderly Andhra woman who does most of the cooking at our home. And she makes this dish quite often, especially when there is leftover rice. The best part of this dish is that it tastes good the next day as well.

Ingredients

4 tablespoons Tamarind Pulp (see below)

1½ cups rice, soaked

¼ teaspoon turmeric powder

Salt to taste

2 tablespoons oil

½ teaspoon mustard seeds

1 teaspoon skinless split black gram

1 teaspoon split Bengal gram

A large pinch of asafoetida

10-15 curry leaves

2 green chillies, finely chopped

2 dried red chillies, broken into large bits

½ cup crushed roasted peanuts

1 teaspoon roasted sesame seeds

Method

1 Cook the rice with the turmeric powder, salt and three cups of water till tender. Ensure that the rice grains remain separate. Spread out on a plate to cool.

2 Heat the oil in a non-stick pan. Add the mustard seeds, split black gram and Bengal gram, and sauté till the gram turn golden brown. Add the asafoetida, curry leaves, green chillies and red chillies, and sauté till fragrant.

3 Stir in the tamarind pulp diluted in one-fourth cup of water and cook till the mixture thickens. Add the rice and mix gently. Adjust the salt. Add the peanuts and sesame seeds, and mix gently. Serve hot.

Chef's Tip: *Imli chawal* will keep for three to four days and is ideal to carry while travelling.

You can make the tamarind mixture and store it in the refrigerator to use when required.

TAMARIND PULP

Soak 75 grams tamarind in 100 ml warm water for 10-15 minutes. Grind to a smooth paste and strain to remove any fibres. Store in an airtight container in the refrigerator.

SOYA GRANULE RICE

My mother often makes soya granule sabzi which everyone enjoys. Besides, it is full of good proteins. She once made rice with soya granules as a variation, and it was a hit. Actually she had first tasted it at her friend's home and had liked it very much. But she forgot to ask her friend for the recipe and tried out her own version at home. And it turned out fabulous.

Ingredients

1 cup soya granules

1 cup basmati rice, soaked

1 cup milk

3-4 tablespoons ghee

1 inch cinnamon

2-3 green cardamoms

3-4 cloves

½ teaspoon caraway seeds

½ teaspoon cumin seeds

3 medium onions, chopped

1 tablespoon ginger paste

1 tablespoon garlic paste

1 tablespoon coriander powder

¼ teaspoon turmeric powder

1 teaspoon red chilli powder

3-4 large tomatoes, chopped

Salt to taste

2-3 green chillies, chopped

2 tablespoons chopped fresh coriander

½ teaspoon *garam masala* powder

Method

1 Soak the soya granules in milk for half an hour.

2 Heat the ghee in a thick-bottomed non-stick pan; add the cinnamon, cardamoms, cloves, caraway seeds and cumin seeds. When they begin to change colour, add the onions and continue to sauté.

3 Add the ginger paste, garlic paste and a little water and continue to sauté for one minute. Add the coriander powder, turmeric powder, chilli powder and tomatoes, and sauté for another minute. Add the salt and mix.

4 Add the soaked soya granules and green chillies; cover the pan and cook till dry. Add the soaked rice with two cups of water and mix.

5 Add the chopped coriander and *garam masala* powder, and mix well. Cover and cook on low heat till the rice is tender, stirring gently once or twice while the rice is cooking. Serve hot with fresh yogurt.

VEGETABLE THEPLA

*Thepla are a staple in Gujarati homes. My mother-in-law kneads leftover sabzi into the dough.
It is an excellent snack served with chhunda or dahi for kids when they return home from school.
Vandana and Alyona used to come home with a few friends tagging along just for the thepla!*

Ingredients

¼ cup chopped fresh fenugreek

1 medium carrot, grated

¼ medium cabbage, grated

¾ cup wholewheat flour

¼ cup gram flour

1 tablespoon chopped fresh coriander

Salt to taste

¼ teaspoon red chilli powder

¼ teaspoon turmeric powder

½ teaspoon ginger-green chilli paste

1 tablespoon oil + for shallow-frying

Yogurt, as required

Method

1 Mix together the two types of flour with the chopped fenugreek, carrot, cabbage, chopped coriander, salt, chilli powder, turmeric powder, ginger-green chilli paste and one tablespoon of oil.

2 Add enough yogurt to make a semi-soft dough. Divide the dough into twelve equal portions and roll out each portion into a thin *thepla*.

3 Heat a non-stick *tawa* and roast each thepla, drizzling a little oil all around, till both sides are evenly cooked.

4 Serve with *Chhunda* (page 82) or fresh yogurt.

These thepla will last for a minimum of three days since no water is used to make the dough.

MOOLI KE PARANTHE

I have fond memories of these piping hot paranthe straight off the tawa topped with a dollop of melting ghee. The crunchy mooli encased in the crisp folds of the paranthe tastes simply divine.

Ingredients

4 medium white radishes, grated

5-6 tender radish leaves, finely chopped

2½ cups wholewheat flour + for dusting

½ teaspoon carom seeds, crushed

Salt to taste

2 tablespoons ghee + for shallow-frying

1 teaspoon red chilli powder

4 green chillies, chopped

2 tablespoons dried pomegranate seeds, crushed

4 tablespoons fresh coriander leaves, chopped

Squeeze out excess moisture from the radish mixture each time just before stuffing it into the dough portion or the paranthe will turn soggy.

Method

1 Squeeze out the juice from the grated radish and set aside.

2 Mix together the flour, one-fourth teaspoon carom seeds and salt; rub in two tablespoons of ghee with your fingertips.

3 Add enough water and knead into a medium soft dough. Cover with a damp cloth and set aside for fifteen to twenty minutes.

4 To make the filling, combine the radish, radishes leaves, salt, chilli powder, green chillies, remaining crushed carom and pomegranate seeds and chopped coriander in a bowl.

5 Divide the dough into eight equal portions. Flatten each portion, making the edges thinner than the centre.

6 Take one portion of the filling, squeeze out extra moisture and place it in the centre of the flattened dough. Gather the edges of the dough together and roll it into a ball.

7 Press the ball lightly to flatten and roll out into a *parantha* on a greased and floured board or table.

8 Heat a non-stick *tawa*. Place a *parantha* on the *tawa* and cook for one minute. Turn over and drizzle a little ghee over it. Turn over once again and drizzle a little ghee on top. Roast till both sides are golden and crisp on the outside. Serve hot.

Chef's Tip: You can replace the radish with grated cauliflower to make *Gobhi ke Paranthe*.

NAMAK AJWAIN KE PARANTHE

Quick, delicious and excellent for digestion, who can ask for anything more! Serve them with fresh dahi or pickle, as my mother does, and watch them disappear in a flash.

Ingredients

Salt to taste

1½ teaspoons crushed carom seeds *(ajwain)*

3 cups wholewheat flour

2 tablespoons ghee + for shallow-frying

Method

1 Mix together the flour, salt and crushed carom seeds. Rub in two tablespoons of ghee. Add enough water and knead into a medium soft dough. Cover with a damp cloth and set aside for fifteen to twenty minutes.

2 Divide the dough into twelve portions. Roll out each portion into a thick roti. Spread a little ghee over and fold into a semicircle. Fold it once more to make a triangle. Roll out each triangle into a *parantha*.

3 Heat a non-stick *tawa*. Place the *parantha* on it. Turn it over once and drizzle some ghee around. Turn it over again and drizzle a little more ghee around. Cook, turning over a few times, till both sides are well cooked and golden. Serve hot with fresh yogurt and pickle.

Use leftover dal instead of water to knead the dough, and add some chopped onion, green chillies, chilli powder and fresh coriander to make Dal Paranthe.

PYAAZ AUR CHAWAL KE PARANTHE

An experiment that turned out successful! My mother made it the first time at her cousin's home. The lady was unwell and had a house full of guests to feed. So my mother offered to cook breakfast. There were a few leftover vegetables and rice in the refrigerator which she turned into these mouth-watering paranthe. And now we cook extra rice at dinner time so that she can use the leftover rice to make these paranthe for breakfast the next morning!

Ingredients

3 medium onions, chopped

2 cups cooked rice

2½ cups wholewheat flour

Salt to taste

2 tablespoons ghee + for shallow-frying

¼ teaspoon carom seeds

2 green chillies, finely chopped

½ teaspoon red chilli powder

2 tablespoons chopped fresh coriander

Method

1 Mix together the flour and salt; rub in two tablespoons of ghee with your fingertips. Add enough water and knead into a medium soft dough. Cover with a damp cloth and set aside for fifteen to twenty minutes.

2 Mix together the rice, onions, carom seeds, green chillies, chilli powder, chopped coriander and salt.

3 Divide the dough into eight equal portions and roll into balls. Roll out each ball into a thick *puri*. Stuff each *puri* with one portion of the rice mixture and shape into a ball again. Roll out each ball into a seven-inch round *parantha*.

4 Heat a non-stick *tawa*. Place a *parantha* on it. Turn it over once and drizzle some ghee around it. Turn over again and drizzle a little more ghee around. Cook, turning over a few times, till both sides are well cooked and golden brown. Serve hot with fresh yogurt and pickle.

Dal
&
Kadhi

DAL DHOKLI

This was the perfect Sunday lunch in my in-law's home for many years – an easy to prepare one-dish meal: nutritious and a good way to feed protein-rich dal and wholewheat flour to growing children. Don't forget the topping of finely chopped onions, fresh coriander and lemon juice. And, yes, a few drops of pure ghee.

Ingredients

1 cup split pigeon peas, soaked

¾ cup wholewheat flour

¼ cup gram flour

Salt to taste

¾ teaspoon turmeric powder

¾ teaspoon red chilli powder

2 pinches asafoetida

2 tablespoons oil

1½ tablespoons peanuts

2 tablespoons pure ghee

¾ teaspoon mustard seeds

¼ teaspoon fenugreek seeds

2 dried red chillies, broken into large bits

10 curry leaves

1½ teaspoons green chilli paste

1 teaspoon jaggery, grated

1 tablespoon lemon juice

2 tablespoons chopped fresh coriander

1 small onion, finely chopped

Method

1 Mix together the flour and gram flour. Add the salt, one-fourth teaspoon turmeric powder, the chilli powder, a pinch of asafoetida, half a tablespoon of oil and sufficient water to make a stiff dough.

2 Roll out the dough into a thin *roti* and brush a little oil on both sides. Cut into strips, squares or diamonds and set aside.

3 Boil the split pigeon peas with two cups of water, salt and the remaining turmeric powder. Add the peanuts to the *dal* when it is half cooked. Continue to cook till the *dal* is soft. Whisk till smooth.

4 Heat half the ghee in a non-stick pan; add the mustard seeds, fenugreek seeds, remaining asafoetida, red chillies, curry leaves and green chilli paste. When the seeds splutter, add the cooked *dal* and stir.

5 Add two cups of water and bring the mixture to a boil. Add the jaggery and cook till it dissolves. Add the strips of dough and cook, stirring gently occasionally so that the dough does not stick to the bottom of the pan. Adjust the salt.

6 Once the dough strips are cooked, take the pan off the heat. Gently stir in the lemon juice.

7 Serve hot, garnished with the chopped coriander and onion, and drizzle the remaining ghee.

Make extra dal dhokli as the leftovers are delicious with steamed rice.

GUJARATI KADHI

My mother-in-law recalls that while the family was posted in Delhi,
they had a group of Punjabi friends, who used to drink this kadhi by the glassful!
Punjabi kadhi is quite thick and so this light, sweet and sour version was a treat!

Ingredients

2 tablespoons gram flour

2 cups yogurt

1 teaspoon ginger-green chilli paste

Salt to taste

2 teaspoons ghee

½ teaspoon mustard seeds

½ teaspoon cumin seeds

8-10 curry leaves

2 dried red chillies, broken into large bits

A pinch of asafoetida

3-4 cloves

1 inch cinnamon

1 small radish, cut into thin strips

1 small potato, cut into thin strips

1 medium ripe banana, cut into thin round slices (optional)

1 teaspoon sugar

1 tablespoon chopped fresh coriander

Method

1 Whisk together the gram flour, yogurt and ginger-green chilli paste till smooth. Add three cups of water and salt, and mix well. Set aside.

2 Heat the ghee in a deep non-stick pan and add the mustard seeds, cumin seeds, curry leaves, red chillies, asafoetida, cloves and cinnamon. When the seeds splutter, add the radish and potato, and stir to mix. Add one cup of water and cook on medium heat till the vegetables are tender.

3 Add the yogurt mixture and continue to cook, stirring continuously, till the mixture thickens slightly. Adjust the salt. Add the banana and sugar, and mix lightly. Serve hot, garnished with the chopped coriander.

MAA CHOLEYAAN DI DAL

*As children we used to look forward to visiting Gurudwaras especially for the
"langarwali dal" as my mother preferred to call it, as it is always served at a langar.*

Ingredients

⅔ cup split black gram with skin, soaked

⅓ cup split Bengal gram, soaked

Salt to taste

¼ teaspoon turmeric powder

2 tablespoons pure ghee

1 medium onion, chopped

1½ inches ginger, chopped

4-5 garlic cloves, chopped

A large pinch of asafoetida

1 medium tomato, chopped

1 teaspoon red chilli powder

½ teaspoon *garam masala* powder

1 tablespoon chopped fresh coriander

Method

1 Place the split black gram and Bengal gram with four cups of water, salt and turmeric powder in a pressure cooker. Cook under pressure on low heat till the pressure is released four times (four whistles).

2 Heat the ghee in a non-stick pan. Add the onion, ginger, garlic and asafoetida, and sauté till golden. Add the tomato and sauté till it turns soft and pulpy.

3 Add the chilli powder and *garam masala* powder, and sauté till the ghee rises to the surface.

4 Stir in the cooked lentils. Add one cup of water, adjust the salt and simmer for half an hour, or till the lentils are completely soft.

5 Garnish with the chopped coriander and serve hot with *roti* or rice.

The consistency of this dal is quite thick as it is usually eaten with roti. Thin it down with water if you want to eat it with rice.

OSAMAN

Osaman can be made with many different dal, but my mother-in-law prefers making it with sabut moong. What better way to use up moong ka paani than with a light seasoning of curry patta? Don't forget to add lemon juice for a tangy flavour.

Ingredients

1 cup whole green gram

Salt to taste

½ inch ginger

2 green chillies

2 tablespoons ghee

A large pinch of asafoetida

½ teaspoon mustard seeds

½ teaspoon cumin seeds

3-4 cloves

1 inch cinnamon

12 curry leaves

1 teaspoon yogurt, whisked

½ teaspoon turmeric powder

1 teaspoon grated jaggery

2 teaspoons lemon juice

1 tablespoon chopped fresh coriander

Method

1 Wash the gram and soak it in two cups of water for about half an hour. Drain and place in a deep non-stick pan with five cups of fresh water and salt, and bring to a boil. Lower the heat and simmer till completely cooked.

2 Alternatively, pressure-cook the gram with five cups of water till the pressure is released four times (four whistles).

3 Strain the cooked gram and use only the stock. The gram can be used to make some other dish.

4 Grind the ginger and green chillies to a fine paste. Dilute the paste with one tablespoon of water.

5 Heat the ghee in a non-stick pan. Add the asafoetida, mustard seeds and cumin seeds along with the cloves, cinnamon, and curry leaves.

6 When the seeds begin to splutter, add the diluted ginger-green chilli paste, yogurt and salt. Stir in the reserved stock and turmeric powder.

7 When the mixture comes to a boil, adjust the salt and add the jaggery. Cook on low heat for two to three minutes.

8 Just before serving, add the lemon juice and chopped coriander. Serve hot.

PUNJABI PAKOREWALI KADHI

*This is a hot favourite with Alyona and my sister Namrata. These days
everybody is so very health conscious and wants to avoid deep-fried foods,
so my mother makes it with sliced onions instead of the pakore.*

Ingredients

Pakore

1 cup gram flour

1 small onion, chopped

¼ cup chopped fresh fenugreek

½ inch ginger, grated

½ teaspoon carom seeds

½ teaspoon red chilli powder

Salt to taste

Oil for deep-frying

Kadhi

2 cups yogurt

½ cup gram flour

1 teaspoon turmeric powder

Salt to taste

2 tablespoons oil

½ teaspoon fenugreek seeds

½ teaspoon cumin seeds

2 dried red chillies, broken into large bits

½ inch ginger, chopped

1 teaspoon red chilli powder

Method

1 For the *pakore,* place the gram flour in a bowl. Add the onion, fenugreek leaves, ginger, carom seeds, chilli powder and salt, and mix. Add about one-fourth cup of water and mix well.

2 Heat sufficient oil in a non-stick *kadai;* drop small portions of the mixture into the hot oil and deep-fry till golden brown. Drain on absorbent paper and set aside.

3 For the *kadhi,* whisk the yogurt well. Add the gram flour and whisk thoroughly till smooth. Add the turmeric powder, salt and three cups of water and mix well.

4 Heat the oil in a non-stick *kadai.* Add the fenugreek seeds, cumin seeds, and red chillies, and sauté for half a minute. Add the ginger and sauté for a minute. Stir in the yogurt mixture, bring to a boil and cook on low heat for about fifteen to twenty minutes, stirring occasionally.

5 Add the chilli powder and fried *pakore,* and continue to simmer for two to three minutes. Serve hot with steamed rice.

Chef's Tip: You can add Rajasthani *gatte* in place of the *pakore.*

RAJMA MASALA

Another favourite of mine. I always ask my mother to make this for me whenever I return from a long business trip. And I enjoy it with hot steamed rice and dahi. You don't need any other side dish.

Ingredients

1 cup kidney beans

Salt to taste

2 medium onions, roughly chopped

4-5 garlic cloves, roughly chopped

2 inches ginger, roughly chopped

3 tablespoons oil

¾ teaspoon red chilli powder

1 teaspoon coriander powder

1 teaspoon turmeric powder

5 medium tomatoes, puréed

½ teaspoon *garam masala* powder

½ teaspoon roasted cumin powder

2 tablespoons chopped fresh coriander

Method

1 Soak the kidney beans overnight in four cups of water. Drain and rinse in fresh water.

2 Add five cups of water and salt to the beans and cook in a pressure cooker till the pressure is released four to five times (four to five whistles).

3 Grind the onions, garlic and ginger to a smooth paste.

4 Heat the oil in a non-stick *kadai*; add the ground paste and sauté till pale gold.

5 Add the chilli powder, coriander powder and turmeric powder, and sauté for two minutes. Stir in the tomato purée and sauté till the oil separates.

6 Stir in the kidney beans with two cups of water and adjust salt. Bring the mixture to a boil, lower the heat and simmer, covered, for about ten minutes.

7 Stir in the *garam masala* powder and roasted cumin powder. Garnish with the chopped coriander and serve hot with steamed rice.

TREVTI DAL

The trio of lentils makes this the perfect winter dish in the North. We like it lavishly seasoned with fried onions and garlic, the way my mother-in-law serves it. It is very filling and excellent with paranthe, roti or jeera rice.

Ingredients

⅓ cup skinless split green gram, soaked

⅓ cup split pigeon peas, soaked

⅓ cup split Bengal gram, soaked

½ teaspoon turmeric powder

1 inch ginger, grated

2 green chillies, slit

1 tablespoon ghee

Salt to taste

2 large onions, finely chopped

½ teaspoon red chilli powder

Add two chopped garlic cloves with the onions for a different flavour.

Method

1 Drain and mix the three lentils and place them in a pressure cooker. Add three cups of water, the turmeric powder, ginger, green chillies, one-fourth teaspoon ghee and salt, and cook under pressure till the pressure is released three times (three whistles), or till completely cooked.

2 Heat the remaining ghee in a non-stick pan; add the onions and sauté till well browned. Stir in the chilli powder and take the pan off the heat.

3 Just before serving, reheat the *dal*, add the sautéed onions and mix well. Serve hot with rice.

Pickles & Chutneys

CHHUNDA

Every year my mother-in-law makes 5 kilos of chhunda and it does not matter which town or country they are in! The recipe is easy to make as there is no cooking involved. This spicy-sweet pickle is especially handy to whip up snacks for hungry kids: serve with thepla, roti or masala puri.

Ingredients

1 kilogram unripe mangoes

2-3 tablespoons salt

½ teaspoon turmeric powder

1 kilogram sugar

2 tablespoons Kashmiri chilli powder

2 tablespoons roasted cumin powder

Method

1 Wash, dry thoroughly, peel and grate the mangoes.

2 Place the grated mangoes in a stainless steel bowl. Add the salt and set aside for one or two hours. Add the turmeric powder and sugar, and mix. Leave to stand overnight.

3 The following day, cover the bowl with a piece of muslin and place it in direct sunlight for six to seven days, or till the sugar dissolves completely and forms a syrup of one-thread consistency. Each day at sunset bring the bowl indoors and stir the mixture with a clean, dry spoon.

4 After seven days, add the chilli powder and roasted cumin powder, and mix well. Stand the jar in the sun for one more day.

5 When it cools down completely, transfer the *chhunda* into a sterilised glass jar with a tight-fitting lid.

Chef's Tip: You can also cook *chhunda* on a stove. After mixing in the turmeric powder and sugar, cook on medium heat till the sugar dissolves and forms a syrup of one-thread consistency. Set aside to cool completely. The next day, add the chilli powder and cumin powder, and mix. Store in a sterilised jar.

AVAKKAI

Another recipe my mother-in-law learnt while my father-in-law was posted at Vishakhapatnam.
They first ate it at a friend's home. Apparently they had never tasted a pickle with garlic before!
My father-in-law loves to eat it with rice. My mother-in-law always makes a bottle of this
every year for me and her grandchildren in Australia.

Ingredients

1 kilogram unripe mangoes

300 grams salt

1 tablespoon turmeric powder

1 cup mustard powder

1 cup red chilli powder

3 cups sesame oil

½ cup garlic cloves, peeled

¼ cup fenugreek seeds

Method

1 Select unblemished, firm, sour mangoes with soft seeds. Wash thoroughly and wipe them completely dry.

2 Cut them in half, remove the soft centre seed letting the hard shell remain. Cut each half into six to eight pieces. Add one tablespoon of salt and the turmeric powder, and mix well. Leave to stand for two hours.

3 Mix together the remaining salt, mustard powder and chilli powder with half a cup of oil. Mix the spices into the mango pieces.

4 Arrange a layer of the mango pieces in a sterilised ceramic jar. Over the mangoes arrange a layer of garlic cloves, sprinkle some fenugreek seeds and drizzle some of the remaining oil. Continue with the layers till all the ingredients are used up, reserving one-fourth cup of oil.

5 Cover the jar with a piece of muslin, fastened with a piece of string around the rim. Store the jar in a cool, dry place for two days. On the third day, add the reserved oil, and cover the jar once again with a piece of muslin fastened around the rim.

6 The pickle will be ready for consumption in a couple of days and will last for a year if stored well.

GAJAR GOBHI SHALGAM KA ACHAAR

This pickle is made by my mother every year during the winter season for it is then that you get the best gajar, gobhi and shalgam.

Ingredients

500 grams carrots, cut into 1½-inch pieces

500 grams cauliflower, separated into medium florets

500 grams turnips, peeled and cut into1½-inch pieces

12 tablespoons mustard oil

6 tablespoons coarsely ground ginger

4 tablespoons coarsely ground garlic

1½ tablespoons mustard seeds, powdered

1½ tablespoons Kashmiri chilli powder

1½ tablespoons Punjabi *Garam Masala*
  Powder (page 44)

1 cup grated jaggery

1½-2 tablespoons salt

3 tablespoons malt vinegar

This pickle keeps well for upto a year and the vegetables do not lose their crunchiness. In fact, as the pickle matures the taste gets enhanced.

Method

1 Heat the oil in a non-stick *kadai*. Add the ground ginger and garlic, and sauté till light golden brown.

2 Add the powdered mustard seeds, chilli powder and *garam masala* powder, and sauté for a few seconds.

3 Add the jaggery and salt, and mix well.

4 Add the vegetables, mix well and cook for three to four minutes. Take the pan off the heat and set aside to cool completely. Stir in the vinegar and mix well. Store in sterilised bottles.

AAM DA ACHAAR

My mother always adds kachcha kabuli chana to this pickle. You can also add karela. Just scrape the outer skin, apply salt and dry the karela in the sun for a day or two. Add the sundried karela to the other ingredients and submerge it in the achaar masala. Then let the pickle mature in the sun. Delicious!

Ingredients

1 kilogram whole unripe mangoes

750 ml filtered mustard oil

250 grams salt

50 grams turmeric powder

50 grams red chilli powder

100 grams crushed fennel seeds

50 grams crushed fenugreek seeds

10 grams onion seeds

200 grams chickpeas

Method

1 Wash and wipe the mangoes completely dry. Cut them in half, remove the soft seed letting the hard shell remain. Cut the mangoes into one-inch cubes.

2 Heat the oil to smoking point. Remove from heat and set aside to cool.

3 Place the mango cubes, salt, turmeric powder, chilli powder, fennel seeds, fenugreek seeds, onion seeds and chickpeas in a large sterilised porcelain jar and mix well. Add half the cooled oil and mix.

4 Cover the jar with a piece of muslin and fasten it around the rim with a piece of string. Place the jar in direct sunlight for three to four days. Remember to mix the contents at least once a day with a clean, dry spoon.

5 Add the remaining oil and let the pickle mature for fifteen days before using.

6 This mango pickle has a shelf life of one year.

Make sure that the pieces of mango are always below the layer of oil, which serves as a preservative.

SWEET LEMON PICKLE

This pickle is another fixture on our pantry shelf. My mother makes bottles of
this pickle in October or November when lemons are freely available and less expensive.

Ingredients

1 kilogram thin-skinned lemons

200 grams salt

50 grams black salt

750 grams sugar

50 grams Punjabi *Garam Masala* Powder (page 44)

50 grams red chilli powder

Method

1 Wash and wipe the lemons thoroughly dry. Slit them into four without cutting
through.

2 Mix together the salt, black salt, sugar, *garam masala* powder and chilli powder. Stuff
the mixture into the lemons.

3 Place the lemons in a porcelain jar. Cover the jar with a piece of muslin, fastened
around the rim with a piece of string. Stand the jar in direct sunlight for about a month.
Remember to mix the contents at least once a day with a clean, dry spoon.

4 The pickle will now be ready for consumption. It can be stored for one year.

To shorten the pickling time,
slice the lemons thinly and mix
with the spices and the pickle
will be ready to consume earlier.
If you make it with whole
lemons, it will take a little
longer to mature.

STUFFED RED CHILLI PICKLE

*My mother first tasted this pickle while visiting Saharanpur and instantly fell
in love with it. When she returned home she tried it out with great success.
Ever since she has been making it every year. It's a hot favourite in our home.*

Ingredients

500 grams large fresh red chillies

650 ml mustard oil

100 grams salt

150 grams fennel seeds, coarsely powdered

50 grams fenugreek seeds, coarsely powdered

50 grams dried mango powder

100 grams mustard seeds, coarsely powdered

50 grams coriander seeds, coarsely powdered

¼ cup vinegar

*Use Benarasi mirchi
for this recipe.*

Method

1 Wash and thoroughly dry the red chillies. Make a slit on one side of the chillies.

2 Heat the oil till smoking point. Set aside to cool.

3 Mix together the salt, fennel powder, fenugreek powder, dried mango powder, mustard powder and coriander powder. Add a little oil and mix to make a firm mixture.

4 Stuff the mixture into the chillies and place them in a porcelain jar. Pour over the remaining oil and vinegar.

5 Cover the jar with a piece of muslin fastened around the rim with a piece of string, and place it in direct sunlight for about a week to ten days.

6 Stir the contents in the jar gently or else the *masala* will come out of the chillies.

7 The pickle will now be ready for consumption. It can be stored for a year.

GOAN CHILLI PICKLE

This is one of my favourites: spread it on bread with butter and it is an instant snack.
As my father-in-law is rather fond of chillies, my mother-in-law had to learn this recipe. In fact, this
was one recipe she has demonstrated the maximum number of times at naval functions. She makes it
in large quantities and gives away small bottles of this pickle as gifts to her friends.

Ingredients

500 grams mild green chillies

8-10 dried red Reshampatti chillies

½ cup salt

1 cup vinegar

250 grams garlic, chopped

200 grams ginger, chopped

½ cup Tamarind Pulp (page 61)

1 cup sesame oil

1 cup sugar

1 teaspoon fenugreek seeds, powdered

Method

1 Crush the green chillies with a little salt in a blender. Soak the red chillies in a little of the vinegar for about half an hour.

2 Crush the garlic and ginger. Grind the red chillies with the rest of the vinegar and the tamarind pulp.

3 Heat the oil in a non-stick pan till smoking point. Cool slightly and add the crushed garlic, ginger, and green chillies. Sauté on high heat for four to five minutes.

4 Add the red chilli paste and sugar, and continue to cook, stirring continuously, for another four to five minutes.

5 Add the remaining salt and stir. Add the powdered fenugreek seeds and mix well. Cook for five to seven minutes. Set aside to cool completely.

6 Transfer into sterilised bottles and store in a refrigerator.

TAMARIND CHUTNEY

Ingredients

1 cup tamarind

1¼ cups grated jaggery

1 inch cinnamon

2 tablespoons raisins

Salt to taste

¼ teaspoon black salt

1 teaspoon red chilli powder

1 teaspoon roasted cumin powder

1½ teaspoons dried ginger powder

Method

1 Remove seeds and soak the tamarind in two cups of warm water for half an hour. Squeeze out the pulp and strain.

2 Cook the tamarind pulp and jaggery in a heavy-bottomed non-stick pan on low heat.

3 Add the cinnamon and cook for fifteen minutes. Add the raisins, salt, black salt, chilli powder, roasted cumin powder and dried ginger powder.

4 Remove from heat and set aside to cool. Store in an airtight container.

GREEN CHUTNEY

Ingredients

1 cup fresh coriander, chopped

½ cup fresh mint, chopped

2-3 green chillies, chopped

Black salt to taste

¼ teaspoon sugar

1 teaspoon lemon juice

Method

1 In a blender, process the chopped coriander and mint with the chopped green chillies. Make a smooth paste using a little water if required.

2 Add the black salt and sugar. Transfer to a bowl and stir in the lemon juice.

Chef's Tip: You can use crushed dried pomegranate seeds or dried mango powder instead of lemon juice. In season unripe green mango is a good substitute.

Variation: Add one cup of yogurt to two tablespoons of chutney for a completely different flavour.

Sweets & Desserts

BADAM-PISTA KULFI

Alyona's Nana was very fond of ice creams and my mother-in-law used to make this kulfi at short notice. In summer, she used to add mango pulp to make mango kulfi. Homemade kulfi is healthier than ice cream and Alyona and her sisters expected the freezer to be stocked with kulfi during their summer vacations!

Ingredients

12-15 almonds, coarsely ground

15-20 pistachios, coarsely ground

1½ litres milk

A pinch of saffron

1 tin (400 grams) sweetened condensed milk

¼ cup *khoya/mawa*, grated

Method

1 Heat the milk in a thick-bottomed non-stick pan. When the milk begins to boil, add the saffron, lower the heat and simmer, stirring continuously, till the milk is reduced by half.

2 Add the condensed milk, almonds and pistachios, and mix well. Cook for three to four minutes, stirring continuously. Take the pan off the heat and set aside to let cool.

3 Add the *khoya* and mix well. Pour into individual *kulfi* moulds and place them in the freezer to set.

4 Unmould and serve immediately.

Keep a jar of equal amounts of ground almonds, pistachios and cardamom handy, which can be added to kulfi and other desserts.

BESAN KA SHEERA

This is an excellent remedy for bad colds as it helps control sneezing. My mother always
makes it whenever anyone has a cold. My father simply loved it and could eat it at any time.
In fact he would say, "Give it to me often so that I do not get a cold ever".

Ingredients

5 tablespoons gram flour

4 tablespoons pure ghee

10-12 almonds, coarsely ground

10 pistachios, coarsely ground

6 tablespoons sugar

2 pinches green cardamom powder

Method

1 Heat the ghee in a non-stick pan; add the gram flour and sauté till brown and fragrant.

2 Add the almonds, pistachios and two cups of water, and keep stirring to prevent lumps from forming.

3 Add the sugar and cardamom powder, and cook till the mixture thickens. Serve hot.

CHOCOLATE BURFI

Another one of my father's favourite dishes. He actually loved to make it himself.
My mother would get the ingredients ready and he would make the burfi himself.

Ingredients

3 tablespoons cocoa powder

500 grams *khoya/mawa*

Oil, for greasing

⅓ to ½ cup powdered sugar

Edible silver foil (optional)

Method

1 Crumble the *khoya* into fine granules. Grease a tray with the oil and set aside.

2 Cook the *khoya* in a thick-bottomed non-stick pan, stirring continuously, till it has completely melted and has a thick sauce-like consistency. Make sure that it does not change colour.

3 Remove from heat and leave to cool slightly. Add the powdered sugar and mix well.

4 Pour half the mixture onto the greased tray. To spread the *khoya* evenly on the tray, hold the tray at two ends and tap it firmly on a hard surface two or three times. Set aside to cool.

5 Place the remaining mixture on low heat. Add the cocoa powder and mix well.

6 Pour the cocoa mixture over the mixture in the tray and spread evenly.

7 Set aside to cool completely. Cut into pieces and serve, covered with edible silver foil, if desired.

KESARI SHRIKHAND

This is quick and easy to make and tastes delicious eaten with puri.
On a trip to Australia to visit her daughter Vandana, my mother-in-law
found several half-used tubs of yogurt in her refrigerator. She promptly turned
them into shrikhand to the delight of her son-in-law.

Ingredients

A generous pinch of saffron

1 kilogram yogurt

1 cup powdered sugar

2 tablespoons warm milk

A small pinch of nutmeg powder

¼ teaspoon green cardamom powder

5-6 almonds, blanched, peeled and sliced

8-10 pistachios, blanched, peeled and sliced

The same mixture of powdered almonds, pistachios and green cardamom that is used for the Badam-Pista Kulfi can be added with saffron to the drained yogurt.

Method

1 Tie the yogurt in a piece of muslin and hang it overnight over a bowl, in a refrigerator, to drain out the whey.

2 Transfer the drained yogurt into a bowl. Add the powdered sugar and mix well till the sugar dissolves completely.

3 Soak the saffron in the warm milk; cool and add to the yogurt mixture. Mix well.

4 Add the nutmeg powder and cardamom powder, and mix well. Place in a refrigerator to chill.

5 Serve chilled, garnished with the almonds and pistachios.

Chef's Tip: Serve with chopped fresh fruit such as pineapple and mango.

MANGO ICE CREAM

This is the answer to every mother's prayer – a delicious ice cream that can be turned out in a jiffy.
As there are no ice crystals and it is so quick to prepare, it is one of my personal favourites.
Another recipe perfected by my mother-in-law.

Ingredients

1 cup mango purée
1 cup milk
1 cup fresh cream
1 cup milk powder
½ cup powdered sugar

Method

1 Place the milk, fresh cream, milk powder, powdered sugar and mango purée in a blender and blend till smooth.

2 Pour into an ice cream container with a tight-fitting lid and freeze till set. Serve in scoops or slices.

NARIYAL BURFI

After a pooja at her home, my mother-in-law noticed that there were a lot of coconuts. So she had them grated and cooked them with sugar to make burfi. Sometimes, she makes it two-coloured, yellow and white, for Diwali and Bhai Dooj. She once added tomato purée and the colour turned out to be delightful and so did the taste.

Ingredients

2½ cups grated coconut

1 tablespoon ghee, add + for greasing

1½ cups sugar

½ cup milk

¼ teaspoon green cardamom powder

Chef's Tip:
Use a special coconut grater to get fine delicate curls of coconut, which will enhance the appearance of the *burfi*. Add some mango pulp to the coconut to make mango coconut *burfi*.

Method

1 Grease a tray with a little ghee.

2 Mix together the coconut, sugar, milk and cardamom powder in a thick-bottomed non-stick pan and cook on medium heat for ten minutes.

3 Add the ghee and continue to cook till the mixture dries a little and begins to leave the sides of the pan.

4 Pour the mixture onto the greased tray and spread evenly. Cool and cut into pieces and serve.

CUSTARD JELLY WITH FRESH FRUIT

The pieces of fruit peeping through the transparent jelly look inviting. This is a hot favourite with our kids and they often ask their Dadi to make it for them.

Ingredients

4 tablespoons vanilla custard powder

1 packet (200 grams) raspberry jelly

2½ cups milk

4 tablespoons sugar

1 apple, chopped

1 banana, chopped

Method

1. Mix the custard powder in the milk. Heat, stirring continuously. Add sugar and cook, stirring continuously, till the mixture comes to a boil and thickens. Set aside to cool. Pour into individual bowls and chill.

2. Prepare the jelly according to the instructions on the packet and set aside to cool.

3. Mix in the chopped fruit and place in the refrigerator to set.

4. Heap spoonfuls of fruit jelly on the custard and serve immediately.

MOHANTHAAL

*Come Diwali and our household is buzzing with cries of 'chalo mithai banaayen'!
And then my mother-in-law takes over the kitchen. Besan laddoo, anarase
and mohanthaal are three fixtures on our Diwali menu.*

Ingredients

2 cups coarse gram flour

1½ tablespoons + ¾ cup ghee

3 tablespoons milk

1½ cups sugar

5-6 saffron threads

¼ teaspoon green cardamom powder

A large pinch of nutmeg powder

10 almonds, blanched and slivered

10 pistachios, blanched and slivered

Method

1 Place the gram flour in a bowl. Heat a non-stick pan, add one and a half tablespoons of ghee and two tablespoons of milk and warm slightly.

2 Add this to the gram flour and mix with your fingertips till the mixture resembles breadcrumbs. Pass through a thick sieve to get a smooth mixture.

3 Grease a *thali*. Soak the saffron in one tablespoon of warm milk for ten minutes.

4 Heat the remaining ghee in a thick-bottomed non-stick pan. Add the gram flour mixture and cook on medium heat till fragrant and darker in colour.

5 Add half the cardamom powder and nutmeg powder to the gram flour and mix. Take the pan off the heat and keep stirring till the mixture cools completely.

6 Meanwhile, in a separate non-stick pan, cook the sugar and half a cup of water to make a syrup of one-and-a-half-string consistency. Add the saffron-flavoured milk to the sugar syrup and mix well.

7 Add the syrup to the gram flour mixture and stir continuously, till all the liquid has been absorbed and the mixture thickens and becomes a little dry.

8 Pour the mixture into the *thali* and spread evenly till the top is smooth. Sprinkle the almonds, pistachios and the remaining cardamom powder on top and set aside to cool. Cut into squares and serve.

Add khoya to give the mohanthaal a richer texture.

Chef's Tip: If the gram flour mixture dries up too much while cooking, sprinkle a little milk and stir well.

GLOSSARY

English	Hindi	English	Hindi
Almonds	Badam	Jaggery	Gur
Asafoetida	Hing	Kidney beans	Rajma
Black peppercorns	Kali mirch	Ladies' fingers	Bhindi
Black salt	Kala namak	Lotus roots	Kamal kakdi/bhen
Bottle gourd	Lauki		
Broad beans	Sem	Millet	Bajra
Button mushrooms	Khumb	Mustard seeds	Rai/sarson
Capsicum	Shimla mirch	Nutmeg	Jaiphal
Cardamoms, green	Chhoti elaichi	Peanuts/ground nuts	Moongphali
Carom seeds	Ajwain	Peas, pigeon split	Toovar dal/arhar dal
Chickpeas	Kabuli chana		
Cinnamon	Dalchini	Pistachio	Pista
Colocasia	Arbi	Pomegranate seeds, dried	Anardana
Cottage cheese	Paneer	Purple yam	Kand
Cumin seeds	Jeera	Radish	Mooli
Dried mango powder	Amchur	Red lentils, split	Masoor dal
Edible silver foil	Chandi ka varq	Red pumpkin	Kaddu
Fennel seeds	Saunf	Round gourd	Tinda
Fenugreek leaves	Methi	Saffron	Kesar
Fenugreek seeds	Methi dana	Semolina	Rawa/sooji
French beans	Farsi	Sesame seeds	Til
Fresh coriander	Hara dhania	Shallots	Chhote pyaaz
Fresh mint	Pudina	Soda bicarbonate	Khane ka soda
Gram flour	Besan	Spinach	Palak
Gram, Bengal split	Chana dal	Spring onion	Hara pyaaz
Gram, black split	Chilkewali urad dal	Tamarind	Imli
		Turmeric	Haldi
Gram, green skinless split	Dhuli moong dal	Turnip	Shalgam
		Vinegar	Sirka
Gram, whole green	Sabut moong	Wholewheat flour	Atta
Green peas	Matar	Yam	Suran
Jackfruit	Kathal	Yogurt	Dahi